KENNETH S. ALBIN

Tabernacles

It's a Celebration & Not Just an Option

TABERNACLES: IT'S A CELEBRATION & NOT JUST AN OPTION!

How Christians can celebrate this Biblical Feast and the True Birthday of Messiah

BY

Kenneth S. Albin

For more information about Kenneth S. Albin

www.savethenations.com
www.hitthemarktorah.tv

TABLE OF CONTENTS

DESCRIPTIONS

WHAT ARE THE MOEDIM?

The Moedim are appointed days, rehearsals and special set times that God invites His people to gather as a congregation to meet with Him, their Creator and King. In God's sovereignty He has chosen, from the beginning of creation, seven appointed times during His calendar year.

WHAT IS THE SABBATH?

God has also, in His sovereignty, chosen another day that is set apart from the rest. God has pre-determined, by His sovereignty, to set apart the seventh day as the Sabbath for man to rest and to honor the Creator. The Sabbath was created for all of mankind, not just the Jew, Israel, but for all mankind.

WHAT IS A CHRISTIAN?

The word Christian is mentioned three times in the New Testament. It is the Greek word *Christianos*. The term means "to be a little Christ" or "anointed". The term is used to point to a true disciple of Jesus Christ. A Christian is committed to following Jesus Christ, His teachings, His ways and His commands. The disciple of Christ will become more and more like Jesus as the Holy Spirit continues to work and conform their lives to the will of God. A real Christian has been born again and passed from death to life and darkness to the kingdom of Light. (Acts 11:26, Acts 26:28, 1 Peter 4:16, John 5:24, Colossians 1:13,)

WHO ARE THE JEWS?

The word Jew is a term used to describe those from the Southern Kingdom, tribe of Judah or the house of Judah. A Jew may also be from the tribe of Benjamin since that was the tribe given to David's descendants by the prophet Ahijah when he divided the two kingdoms and gave ten tribes to Jeroboam and two tribes to Solomon's son, Rehoboam. In the Southern Kingdom of Judah there were also some from the tribe of Levi and remnants of other tribes. Later these from the Southern House of Israel would also be known as being Jews or Jewish. The title Jew was first used in the bible just before, during and then following the captivity in Babylon. You can see this in the book of Esther and the books of Ezra and Nehemiah. The Northern Kingdom with ten tribes became commonly known as the house of Israel.

WHAT IS A GENTILE?

The term *Gentile* comes from the Hebrew word *Goy* or its plural *Goyim*. It refers to the nations who were not physical descendants of Israel. A Gentile can also be used of the house of Israel, sometimes known as Ephraim, who lost their inheritance and identity when they, in their apostasy and divorce from Yahweh, were scattered to the nations, never to return. They are commonly referred to as the lost tribes of Israel. When a person accepts Jesus, he is "grafted-in" to Israel and becomes connected to and a descendant of Abraham by faith. It is important to understand that a Christian and follower of Jesus is no longer a Gentile. (2 Kings 17:23, Ephesians 2:11-19)

WHAT IS A HEBREW?

A *Hebrew* is the term meaning "one from beyond" or "crossed over one". It refers to Abram who crossed over the Euphrates River into a land that was promised by the God who revealed Himself as the true and living God. Abram crossed over spiritually to forsake his father's idols and worship El Shaddai.

WHAT IS A HEBREW CHRISTIAN?

Though the term Hebrew is not common or usually connected to Christians, but it should be. A Christian is a person who has crossed over from death to life and from darkness to light. This person is a disciple of Jesus Christ and follows His teachings. The term Messiah or Messianic is actually synonymous to the word Christian. Both words come are derived from anointed one from what the Jews call Mashiach or Messiah.

A Hebrew Christian is a person who also embraces their inheritance and identity in connection to Abraham. The Hebrew Christian understands that they are not separated from, but supernaturally connected to Israel through the blood of Jesus & His death, burial and resurrection. The Hebrew Christian receives by faith the benefits of that rich tree and identity. A Hebrew Christian because of grace and truth receives a new identity and inheritance and now gets to walk in the light of the Torah by the power of the Holy Spirit.

In no way is a Christian or a Hebrew Christian ever to think they replace natural Israel or the Jewish people. This is a dangerous and demonic doctrine that has caused many to horrors in the past. The Hebrew Christian is no longer hacked and no longer has their identity and inheritance stolen. They begin to see the Shalom of God working mightily "Nothing Missing, Nothing Broken, Nothing Lost, All Restored!"

WHAT IS TORAH?

Most commonly this refers to the first five books of the Bible known as the Pentateuch. The Torah can also refer to the entire Old Testament known as the Tanakh. Many think it means "law" or a book of "do's and don'ts", but this incorrect. The truest understanding of Torah is "instruction and teaching". The root word for Torah is *yarah* and it is an archery term meaning, "to hit the mark".

Throughout the Scriptures the promise of good things, life and well-being is connected and given to those who obey

Torah. The New & Old Testament word for *sin* means "to miss the mark". So when we obey Torah we "hit the mark" and live well, but when we sin by disobeying the Torah we get the consequences. The Torah, God's Voice and God's Word are all synonymous. (Deuteronomy 4:40, 5:29, Proverbs 6:23, Psalm 119:105)

INTRODUCTION

I hope the title of this book caught your attention, but also did not offend you. When we talk about something not being optional, we are saying that choice is being eliminated. When God created us, He made us very distinct from the animals, as we have the innate ability to reason and to make conscious choices based on our thoughts and intellect. The Scriptures are very clear that with each choice there are consequences. So, when I say it's not optional to celebrate Tabernacles, I am not saying you don't have a choice, but rather hinting at a specific passage in the Bible that in a future date all nations and all people will be required by God to keep this appointed time in Jerusalem. Those who don't do it will wish they did, for life and blessing for the land and the people will be released or withheld based on those decisions.

When we are very young, our choices are either non-existent or very minor. When we get older, with each year comes the ability to choose more options, but with them also come ramifications for those choices. God never wants His people to make the wrong choices.

However, He will not impose His will and best upon those who choose wrong.

If you are from the United States a great deal of emphasis is placed on the rights of its citizens to choose and be free. With freedom of choice also comes a responsibility to use that liberty for blessing and good. The Feast of Tabernacles is the highlight and the last of the Feasts of the Lord. It is the seventh feast and it lasts seven days plus one additional and separate eighth day. Those who would have seen and been a part of this feast in the time of Jesus would no doubt be included in a celebration and party that is hard for us to imagine. There is much to learn from the teachings of the Bible as well as the richness of the traditions that are done. Feast of Tabernacles is a time of celebration and thanksgiving! It is to remind us of God's wonderful presence all around us. It is a special time when we thank God for the harvest we had this year and the greater harvest which is to come. It is to remind us of our future wedding with Christ; the Bride and the Bridegroom coming together for the wedding feast and consummation of their marriage.

Why a tabernacle? It is to remind us that our physical lives, possessions and all we have here on the earth is temporary. We are to trust in the Creator, our heavenly Father for the eternal and spiritual. It points us to look up like Israel who were under the cloud and the pillar of fire that protected Israel on their journey. It helps us see that our lives on earth are fragile and only God can sustain us, only God can protect us and everything we have is really from Him.

Did you know there are many names for this feast?

Feast of Tabernacles
Sukkot
Feast of Booths
Feast of Dedication
Feast of the Nations
Feast of Ingathering
Season of Rejoicing
First fruits of the Grapes

Whatever it is called is not as important as what it represents and means. For when you celebrate this divine appointment you are reminded that your life is temporary and everything you have comes as a blessing from God. God is the Creator and eternal. You are sustained by His goodness and it is ultimately Jesus, the Word, which is the permanence and stability in your life.

In this book we will look at each of these names and see how they will draw us closer to God as we see that Jesus is the ultimate highest expression and point of everything the Torah teaches.

As we begin to look at this special time, I hope you won't wait for the time when it is not optional to celebrate it. Let's begin!

CHAPTER ONE:

"Yahweh-Elohim is My Tabernacle"

The first time Tabernacles is mentioned in the Bible is actually before the giving of the Torah instructions in the desert at Mount Sinai. But before we look at that, let's begin by looking back at Leviticus twenty-three, for it is the framework and guideline for all the seven Moedim of the Lord.

The Moedim are set times, appointments, rehearsals and reminders. They are Yahweh's invitations to be with Him and to celebrate. Each Moed has powerful and prophetic pictures of the past, present and the future for us to discover as we walk in the spirit and truth they illuminate. We must learn, not just by study, but also by experience, for as we celebrate and keep them we will see their mysteries unfold with great blessings.

Make up your mind as you journey to allow the Holy Spirit to be the One to guide you and bring you into

"Divine Alignment with the Divine Assignment" that God has for you. This means being open to getting on God's calendar and Moedim, even if you have never done them before.

Don't let the tradition of your past of what you did and didn't do keep you from starting new traditions that align with what God had set in order from the beginning. As you walk on this journey, some might not understand or wonder why you have to do these new things. Please understand, you don't have to do them; you get to do them as you have been grafted-in to the rich heritage of the stock of Israel and, through Christ, you are a descendant of Abraham.

Once you know your identity and inheritance you will gradually make the transition in line with whole Bible rather than just man's "tradition". So, let's look at the framework of this from Leviticus first and see what we can learn.

Leviticus 23:23-36 NKJV
33 Then the Lord spoke to Moses, saying, 34 "Speak to the children of Israel, saying: 'The fifteenth day of this seventh month shall be the Feast of Tabernacles for seven days to the Lord. 35 On the first day there shall be a holy convocation. You shall do no customary work on it. 36 For seven days you shall offer an offering made by fire to the Lord. On the eighth day you shall have a holy convocation, and you shall offer an offering

made by fire to the Lord. It is a sacred assembly, and you shall do no customary work on it.

Leviticus 23: 42-44 NKJV
39 'Also on the fifteenth day of the seventh month, when you have gathered in the fruit of the land, you shall keep the feast of the Lord for seven days; on the first day there shall be a sabbath-rest, and on the eighth day a sabbath-rest. 40 And you shall take for yourselves on the first day the fruit of beautiful trees, branches of palm trees, the boughs of leafy trees, and willows of the brook; and you shall rejoice before the Lord your God for seven days. 41 You shall keep it as a feast to the Lord for seven days in the year. It shall be a statute forever in your generations. You shall celebrate it in the seventh month. 42 You shall dwell in booths for seven days. All who are native Israelites shall dwell in booths, 43 that your generations may know that I made the children of Israel dwell in booths when I brought them out of the land of Egypt: I am the Lord your God. (Yahweh-Elohim) " 44 So Moses declared to the children of Israel the feasts of the Lord.

Yahweh: "I AM everything you need Me to be whenever you need Me to be it!"

Elohim: The Creator and Sustainer of life, the Strong One,

When God commanded the keeping of the Tabernacles celebration, it was also with a revelation of these two names, Yahweh and Elohim, to Israel. When you understand that in God's names is also His heart, will and identity, you will want to look at them more carefully, at each specific occurrence.

When God revealed His name as Yahweh-Elohim, He was combining His ability to create and sustain with His heart to be whatever you need Him to be in your life. What a powerful and prophetic picture of what is to come. Jesus will be revealed to us in much the same manner, but most people have never been taught about it.

As we look at the Scriptures found here, we can learn some things from them about the Feast of Tabernacles. First of all, it was celebrated on the seventh month and is the seventh and final feast, which occurs in the fall. It starts with seven days and then one connected, but separate, eighth day on the end. This feast is a bookend to Passover, which begins with one day then followed by seven days of Unleavened Bread.

So how does the celebration start? It starts with a Sabbath at the beginning of the first day and a Sabbath on the eight day at the end. We know Sabbath has to do with rest and refreshing and not a time to be burdened with work. So God says, "I want you to start and end with a Sabbath of refreshing" which actually means "*to take a breath.*"

Can you see that God wants you to breathe? He doesn't want you to be burdened and weighed down by life. He has set in His divine plan scheduled down times. Of course, they do you no good unless you receive and take them. David said, "I will take the cup of salvation." God is not against us taking what He has so richly provide. He's a good Father and wants you to enjoy and live the abundant life.

God also wants us to gather during the first and eight day; to gather as a people and to offer sacrifices with fire. As we look more we will see that God instructed the people to take the fruit and leafy branches, palm and the willow tree branches to rejoice before the Lord with. He also asks His people to dwell in booths for seven days as a reminder of Yahweh who brought His people out of Egyptian bondage. This last feast, like all the rest, were the feasts of the Lord and what He wanted for the people to experience and enjoy.

Now, some of you are thinking, "Wow! That is so weird! Why would God want His people to dwell and live in a booth for seven days?" Let's look at the Scriptures and see if we can find an answer.

The first time Tabernacles is mentioned in the Bible, it is called Succoth and was a city.

Genesis 33:17

And Jacob journeyed to Succoth, and built him a house, and made booths (sukkah) for his cattle: therefore the name of the place is called Succoth.

When you want to know the truest meaning of a word or phrase, you must try to find where it is first mentioned in the Bible. The context of this first mention of Succoth is important. You see, Jacob had left his father Isaac's home after stealing his brother Esau's blessing. He had not seen his brother in twenty years and Esau had vowed to kill Jacob when he saw him.

Jacob had wrestled with God in prayer and it was then that God changed his name from Jacob to Israel. Now, as he is on his way, although he is free from deceptive Laban, it will be an encounter with Esau that has kept him up many nights.

However, God intervened and Esau no longer had hatred towards his brother. They reunite and Jacob gives Esau a blessing and then they depart from one another.

Immediately Jacob journeys to Succoth where he decided to build a house, perhaps to have a place that is his own. The building of the house is what David said made him know the Lord had established him as King. Jacob also made booths for his cattle and this is the first time tabernacles and this particular word is used in the

Bible. Note that the word booth is first used to house cattle and not as a house for people.

Sukkah: booth, temporary dwelling, tent, tabernacle
A Sukkah (booth) is made with branches and leaves that are interwoven together for a temporary dwelling and shelter

סֻכָּה çukkâh, sook-kaw'; feminine of H5520; a hut or lair:—booth, cottage, covert, pavilion, tabernacle, tent.

The Sukkah or booth is not a permanent and sturdy structure, but rather something that will be moved or taken down when the journey begins again.

When something is living in the booth, it is exposed to the elements of nature and has the ability to see up into the heavens; the permanence of creation and the sun, the moon and stars. But not the booth, for it is temporary and fragile.

When Israel left Egypt and wandered in the wilderness, the Scripture in Leviticus teaches us that Israel dwelt in these same types of booths until they reached the Promised Land. It was there at night under the stars the children of Israel, the descendants of the one who built the first Sukkah for his cattle, would reflect and remember the miracle of the Exodus from Egypt and how they were being kept and carried by the wings of the Lord.

There are a number of times that we can see that same word for booths or Tabernacles in the Bible. Each time it gives us clues to how God wants us to know His protection, His Provision and the joy He brings to our life in this Moed.

Isaiah 4:6
6 And there will be a tabernacle (sukkah) for shade in the daytime from the heat, for a place of refuge, and for a shelter from storm and rain.

Do you see how the temporary booth and shelter is not to be something we put our trust in? The place of refuge and the shelter from the storm and the rain is a "spiritual sukkah" where God is our shade. So when Israel lived in their booths, they ultimately trusted in Yahweh to be their covering. The physical booth helped remind them of that.

Psalm 31:19-20
19 Oh, how great is Your goodness, which You have laid up for those who fear You, which You have prepared for those who trust in You in the presence of the sons of men! 20 You shall hide them in the secret place of Your presence from the plots of man; You shall keep them secretly in a pavilion (sukkah) from the strife of tongues.

God promises that in His sukkah, it is He alone that keeps us in a secret place and hidden from those who would try to harm us. It is the Lord's goodness that, as we honor His days and appointments, we get to dwell under what He has prepared for His people. God has prepared to protect us even from the strife that comes from the tongues of people. They will not be able to get to us in God's spiritual booth! When we keep and celebrate the Moedim Appointments in the physical realm, we are connecting in a great way in the spiritual realm.

This is how faith works. We do something by faith in response to God's Word and commandments in the natural realm. We do this, it corresponds and connects us to the spiritual realm and blessings already prepared. It is like we are going to the bank of heaven and cashing the spiritual check and promise from Yahweh Himself.

What we do on the earth is necessary or Jesus would not have come in the flesh to die, be buried and rise again. He had to physically do those things to break the curse that was manifesting in the physical. Adam disobeyed God and brought into the natural world a disorder that Christ, the second Adam, reversed as He obeyed in the physical realm.

Psalm 27:5 NKJV
For in the time of trouble (bad, evil, distress) he shall hide me in his pavilion: (a root word for sukkah) in the secret of his tabernacle shall he hide me; he shall set me up upon a rock.

סָכַךְ çâkak, saw-kak'; or שָׂכַךְ sâkak; (Exodus 33:22), a primitive root; properly, to entwine as a screen; by implication, to fence in, cover over, (figuratively) protect:—cover, defence, defend, hedge in, join together, set, shut up. To weave or interweave, especially boughs to make a hedge

A major blessing of the Feast of Tabernacles will be divine protection, but there is also much more in this special time. During this season we are also carried to new heights as we stand upon the Rock that is Christ, the Word.

Cakah the root word of Sukkah in the Hebrew means: To protect, to defend, to screen or to cover by a weave or interweaving

Psalm 139:13 NAS
For Thou didst form my inward parts; Thou didst weave *cakak* me in my mother's womb.

Psalm 5:11ESV
But let all who take refuge in you rejoice; let them ever sing for joy, and spread your protection *cakak* over them, that those who love your name may exult in you.

Psalm 91:1, 4 NHEB
1He who dwells in the secret place of the Most High will rest in the shadow of Shaddai. 4He will cover *cakak* you with his feathers. Under his wings you will take refuge. His faithfulness is a shield and a wall.

Psalm 140:7 NKJV
O GOD the Lord, the strength of my salvation, thou hast covered *cakak* my head in the day of battle (weapons, armed men).

It is during this appointed time on God's calendar He wants to remind us that He is your protector, defender and covering. What man builds is temporary, what God builds is eternal. Even your body is also a temporary booth for your spirit and God's spirit to dwell in.

2 Corinthians 5:1-5 TLV
For we know that if the tent, our earthly home, is torn down, we have a building from God—a home not made with human hands, eternal in the heavens. 2 For in this we groan, longing to be clothed with our heavenly dwelling— 3 if indeed, after we have put it on, we will not be found naked. 4 For we groan while we are in this tent—burdened because we don't want to be unclothed but to be clothed, so that what is mortal may be swallowed up by life. 5 Now the One who prepared us for this very purpose is God, who gave us the Ruach (Spirit) as a pledge.

The Feast of Tabernacles is a reminder to God's covenant people to not be consumed with the temporary and the cares of life, but to remember the Eternal God, who is the source of all blessing.

1 Timothy 6:17 ISV
Tell those who are rich in this age not to be arrogant and not to place their confidence in anything as uncertain as riches. Instead, let them place their confidence in God, who lavishly provides us with everything for our enjoyment

Deuteronomy 8:10-18 LB
10 When you have eaten your fill, bless the Lord your God for the good land he has given you. 11 "But that is the time to be careful! Beware that in your plenty you don't forget the Lord your God and begin to disobey him. 12-13 For when you have become full and prosperous and have built fine homes to live in, and when your flocks and herds have become very large, and your silver and gold have multiplied, 14 that is the time to watch out that you don't become proud and forget the Lord your God who brought you out of your slavery in the land of Egypt. 15 Beware that you don't forget the God who led you through the great and terrible wilderness with the dangerous snakes and scorpions, where it was so hot and dry. He gave you water from the rock! 16 He fed you with manna in the wilderness (it was a kind of bread unknown before) so that you would become humble and so that your trust in

him would grow, and he could do you good. 17 He did it so that you would never feel that it was your own power and might that made you wealthy. 18 Always remember that it is the Lord your God who gives you power to become rich, and he does it to fulfill his promise to your ancestors.

Those of us who have seen so much of God's blessings must make sure we don't put our trust in what we have rather than the One who gave it to us. There is something about living in a temporary booth that would have to affect those dwelling in them for those seven days. Their perspective would no doubt be altered about what is really important in life and where the protection and blessings really come from.

This life is fragile and temporary and we too, are just a vapor, here for a moment and then gone. We must see Yahweh-Elohim as the One who creates life, sustains life and is our source of blessing and goodness.

Yahweh-Elohim is what gives our life meaning and true stability. Without Him, whatever we establish is on the sand. He is the One that sets us upon the Rock and protects us from all harm. Say this with me: "Yawheh-Elohim is my Tabernacle."

God had made a provision for His people that every seven years they would be released from debt. Did you know it was on Tabernacles that this was to be done?

The release or the "shemittah" in Hebrew was a commanded rest for the land and a release of all debt for God's people.

During the seven day Tabernacles celebration, the Torah was to be read before all present; the men, women, children, native born and strangers, so that they could all learn how to fear the Lord and live in blessing when they crossed over into the Promised Land. The Tabernacles blessing is a time to give a first fruit offering and then receive your release of debts and instructions as a spiritual Hebrew who has crossed over out of darkness and into the promised blessings of our inheritance. I pray, in Jesus' name, you receive your release and cancellation of debt by faith right now.

Deuteronomy 31:10-13
10 And Moses commanded them, saying: "At the end of every seven years, at the appointed time in the year of release, at the Feast of Tabernacles, 11 when all Israel comes to appear before the Lord your God in the place which He chooses, you shall read this law before all Israel in their hearing. 12 Gather the people together, men and women and little ones, and the stranger who is within your gates, that they may hear and that they may learn to fear the Lord your God and carefully observe all the words of this law, 13 and that their children, who have not known it, may hear and learn to fear the Lord your God as long as you live in the land which you cross the Jordan to possess.

CHAPTER ONE:

Personal and Small Group Study

Describe the first mention of the word tabernacles and what it meant.

_____

_____

_____

_____

_____

_____

_____

_____

_____

Yahweh: "I AM _____ you need Me to be
_____ you need Me to be it!"

Elohim: The _____ and _____ of life, the Strong One,

How many Feasts of the Lord are there?

_____

Tabernacles is the _____ of the final Fall Feasts.

A major blessing of the Feast of Tabernacles will be divine _____.

A _____ (booth) is made with branches and leaves that are _____ together for a _____ dwelling and _____.

So, when Israel lived in their _____ they ultimately trusted in _____ to be their _____ and the _____ booth helped remind them of that.

Psalm 31:19-20
19 Oh, how great is Your _____, Which You have laid up for those who _____ You, Which You have _____ for those who

_____ in You In the presence of the sons of men!

It is during this _____ time on God's calendar, He wants to remind us that He is our _____, _____ and _____.

What man builds is _____, what God builds is _____.

Tabernacles reminds God's _____ people not to be _____ with the _____ and the_____ of life, but to remember the Eternal God who is the _____ of all blessing.

1 Timothy 6:17 ISV
Tell those who are _____in this age not to be arrogant and not to place their _____ in anything as uncertain as _____. Instead, let them place their _____ in God, who lavishly _____ us with _____ for our enjoyment.

In what ways could you see that celebrating Tabernacles could be a blessing or teach you?

_____

_____

_____

_____

_____

_____

_____

_____

_____

God had made a provision for His people that every
_____ years they would be
_____ from _____.

CHAPTER TWO:

A Feast of Nations

John 1:14 YLT
And the Word became flesh, and did tabernacle among us, and we beheld his glory, glory as of an only begotten of a father, full of grace and truth.

When Jesus came to the earth in flesh, His earthly body was a type of booth and tabernacle. He became flesh for our benefit so, as a man He could break the curse and the power of death that Adam and Eve opened the door to. Now this season is the climax of the year.

It is also a time when the Israelites knew it was more about the nations than it was about them. God had chosen Israel and set His love upon them, not because they were so special, but because He chose to love them. It is this same love that God told them to have for the stranger, and the love that He loved the world with.

Deuteronomy 10:19 AMP

19 Therefore love the stranger and sojourner, for you were strangers and sojourners in the land of Egypt.

The first time love is used in the Bible is when God told Abraham to take his only son, whom he loves, and offer him as a sacrifice on the mountain God tells him. This story is a picture of the love of Father God and His only Son, Jesus, who are both willing to lay down everything for us. It is the price and true cost of love. This is the love that will be demonstrated on the Feast of the Nations.

Genesis 22:2 AMP
[God] said, Take now your son, your only son Isaac, whom you love, and go to the region of Moriah; and offer him there as a burnt offering upon one of the mountains of which I will tell you.

Burnt offerings were love offerings! It was and offering that was to be totally consumed by fire. God is a Consuming Fire and a jealous God. His fire is part of His passion and love.

The Bible tells us very plainly the love we are to have for the stranger is a love that is willing to treat them like you want to be treated. So when Israel would be celebrating the Feast of Tabernacles, they knew they were to demonstrate love to the stranger.

God takes no pleasure in the death of the wicked; only that they should turn and repent. On this day, the light and goodness of God will shine brightly so the nations can come into covenant with Yahweh God.

Leviticus 19:33-34 AMP
33 And if a stranger dwells temporarily with you in your land, you shall not suppress and mistreat him.34 But the stranger who dwells with you shall be to you as one born among you; and you shall love him as yourself, for you were strangers in the land of Egypt. I am the Lord your God.

Ger: sojourner, a temporary inhabitant, a newcomer lacking inherited rights, of foreigners in Israel, though conceded rights, guests

According to the Word, if Israel was a stranger in Egypt, then so were we. As believers we can trace our ancestry to Abraham who was a Hebrew. As Abraham's descendants we were all strangers without a covenant at one time. The Feast of Nations reminds us to entertain strangers and invite them into covenant with a loving God.

Did you know that part of the tradition of Tabernacles is that each night you invite guests to eat with your family in the Sukkah and show them light and love?

What a picture of the heart of God who loved the
stranger and the world.

John 3:16-21 AMP

16 For God so greatly loved and dearly prized the world
that He [even] gave up His only begotten (unique) Son,
so that whoever believes in (trusts in, clings to, relies
on) Him shall not perish (come to destruction, be lost)
but have eternal (everlasting) life.

17 For God did not send the Son into the world in order
to judge (to reject, to condemn, to pass sentence on) the
world, but that the world might find salvation and be
made safe and sound through Him.

18 He who believes in Him [who clings to, trusts in,
relies on Him] is not judged [he who trusts in Him
never comes up for judgment; for him there is no
rejection, no condemnation—he incurs no damnation];
but he who does not believe (cleave to, rely on, trust in
Him) is judged already [he has already been convicted
and has already received his sentence] because he has
not believed in and trusted in the name of the only
begotten Son of God. [He is condemned for refusing to
let his trust rest in Christ's name.]19 The [basis of the]
judgment (indictment, the test by which men are
judged, the ground for the sentence) lies in this: the
Light has come into the world, and people have loved
the darkness rather than and more than the Light, for
their works (deeds) were evil. 20 For every wrongdoer
hates (loathes, detests) the Light, and will not come out
into the Light but shrinks from it, lest his works (his

deeds, his activities, his conduct) be exposed and reproved.21 But he who practices truth [who does what is right] comes out into the Light; so that his works may be plainly shown to be what they are—wrought with God [divinely prompted, done with God's help, in dependence upon Him].

I hope you can see that God's will is for no one to be lost or go to hell. The truth of God is revealed through Jesus. He has come to save and to save the lost, whoever and wherever they are.
The only way a person will die in their sin is when they reject the way and Lordship of Jesus because they love darkness too much to leave it. God's will and His mercy is extended to save, but it must be received. A gift does no one good until it is recognized, received and respected.

Jesus came to save the nations. This Moed of Sukkot is also known as the Feast of Nations. This is a seven-day feast plus one additional separate day. The last eighth day is symbolic of the new heaven and new earth that will be created after the thousand year millennial reign of Christ. Eight is the number of new beginnings. It is also a combination of the number one and seven.

On the Feast of Nations there are specific offerings that were to be given. The total of those offerings equal seventy. The number seventy is very important. It is the number of additional disciples who followed Jesus. It is also the number of years the house of Judah spent in Babylon. It is the number of the sons of Israel who went down into Egypt as a small remnant seed of a family and then left as a mighty nation of millions.

The number seventy is also ten times seven. Ten, we know, can mean law, justice or judgment. Seven is a completion and also rest and refreshing. Seventy represents the nations of the world. It is these nations that Jesus came to save. This is also the focus of the Feast of Tabernacles and Nations. God wants to be the Tabernacle that everyone is living in.

For seven days during this feast, offerings are brought to the Temple. There would be 182 sacrifices for offerings by fire during this week. All of these are divisible by seven. According to Number 29:12-32, this is how it was done:

70 Bulls – 13 bulls would be sacrificed on the first day; 12 on the second; 11 on the third, etc. until the seventh day when the last 7 bulls would be sacrificed.
14 Rams – 2 rams each day.
98 Lambs – 14 lambs each day.

In addition to these sacrifices there would have been grain offerings, sin offerings and drink offerings.

We know from the following Scriptures that, at that time in history, there were 70 nations.

Exodus 1:1:5
5 The descendants of Jacob numbered seventy in all; Joseph was already in Egypt.

Genesis 46:27 NIV
27 With the two sons who had been born to Joseph in Egypt, the members of Jacob's family, which went to Egypt, were seventy in all.

Deuteronomy 32:8
When the Most High gave the nations their inheritance, when he divided all mankind, he set up boundaries for the peoples according to the number of the sons of Israel.

God spoke to Israel many times in His Word and basically said, "Salvation is not only for you, because when Messiah comes, He will be for all nations."

During this feast, the priests would be making sacrifices for the salvation of every nation. It was a prophetic act that pointed to Jesus who would die for the lost sheep of the house of Israel and to save the nations. At a certain time they would cry out, "Oh, God, save the nations!" and the special ceremony would take place. It is filled with types and shadows of Jesus.

On Sukkot, all priests in Jerusalem would gather at the Temple. The nations would also be welcomed to come to the Temple during this time. The priests and Levites who worked in the Temple were then divided into three distinct groups:

1st group- these were on festival duty and prepared sacrifices for the offering at the Temple

2nd group- they go out the East gate and gather the willow tree branches from Valley of Motzah

3rd group- (Led by the high priest) they go out the Water Gate to the pool of Siloam (where Jesus healed the blind man); the high priest gathers "living waters" (mayim-chayim in Hebrew) into a golden vase. His assistant would have a silver vase of wine.

At a certain time, the shofar would blow and both groups would begin a synchronized procession towards the Temple.

When the priests walking with willow branches would walk towards the Temple, the branches would make a swishing sound in the wind. This would be symbolic of the Holy Spirit coming upon Jerusalem and the nations because in Hebrew the wind, breath or spirit is the Ruach.

It was so perfectly timed that each distinct group would arrive at the exact moment at their gates. The three would be in perfect harmony and unison.

THE THREE WOULD BECOME AS ONE!

•   A shofar would blow and a flute player (known as "the pierced one") would come & lead the procession into the Temple. The "pierced one" calls for the wind (Holy Spirit) and (living) waters to enter the Temple!

•   The priests would enter with the sacrifices and lay them on the altar. (BLOOD)

•   The priests with willows would enter and circle the altar seven times.

•   The high priest and his assistant would walk up to the altar with the water and the wine.

•   The people present would begin singing the song Mayim, saying, "With joy we will draw water out of the well of salvation [Yeshua]" (Isaiah 12:3)

They are calling for the Messiah to come!

Isaiah 12:2-3
Behold, God is my salvation, I will trust and not be afraid; 'For Yah, the Lord, is my strength and song; He also has become my salvation.'"3 Therefore with joy you will draw water From the wells of salvation (Yeshua).

•   The willow branches are laid on the altar to make a Sukkah or a Wedding Chuppah.

•   The high priest comes in and water is poured into bowl with a small hole on the altar… (Joel 2-God will pour out His Spirit…)

This is the only time water is added to blood and used together. Blood washes sin and water is for cleansing and also is symbolic of life joy, and blessing. Remember the blood & water that poured from Jesus' side?

John 19:34
But one of the soldiers with a spear pierced his side, and forthwith came there out blood and water.

•   The high priest's assistant then comes and pours wine into second bowl. This will be poured into the living water so they mix together. Wine is one symbol of a marriage covenant… "Water into wine."

Remember Jesus' first miracle in Cana was turning water into wine.

John 7:37-39 AMP

(Jesus is celebrating Feast of Booths) 37 Now on the last day, the great day of the feast, Jesus stood and cried out, saying, "If anyone is thirsty, let him come to Me and drink. 38 He who believes in Me, as the Scripture said, 'From his innermost being will flow rivers of living water.'" 39 But this He spoke of the Spirit, whom those who believed in Him were to receive; for the Spirit was not yet given, because Jesus was not yet glorified.

On the other six days the priests circled the altar singing and worshipping. Their worship reaches a mighty crescendo on the seventh day.

Psalm 118:25
Save now, I pray, O LORD; O LORD, I pray, send now prosperity.

They are praying for rain to come!

Hosea 6:3
3 Let us know, Let us pursue the knowledge of the Lord. His going forth is established as the morning; He will come to us like the rain, Like the latter and former rain to the earth.

Psalm 72: 6

He shall come down like rain upon the grass before mowing, Like showers that water the earth.

On the seventh and perfect day, all the people would come in Temple with the "four species" –Three branches (willow, palm, and myrtle) in left hand and a citron in the right. They would wave them in six directions; left and right, front and back, above and beneath. Everything in creation has six sides. Six is also the number of man. The six directions represent that there is no limit from where God brings His blessings. There is also a seventh side; the spiritual side. The number seven means completion and perfection. The seventh side is Holy Spirit. It represents that we are empty vessels until filled with the Holy Spirit.

The "four species" also represent man:

Willow: Branches with leaves that can represent the mouth
Lulav: A green closed palm frond from a date tree: This can represent the Spine
Myrtle: boughs with leaves: this can represent the eyes
Etrog: fruit of a Citron Tree: this can represent the heart

On the last day of the Feast the people circled the altar seven times while crying out "Save us now!" Jesus is there in the Temple as they are crying out, calling for the Messiah.

On that seventh time Jesus is bold and speaks. This happens right after the leaders had questioned if He would be taking His message to the Greeks and the dispersed among the nations. These were actually the same house of Israel that were scattered and swallowed by the nations. Jesus, on the Feast of Nations, announced that He was the Living Waters (*mayim-chayim*) they were all thirsty for.

John 7:35-39
35 Then the Jews said among themselves, "Where does He intend to go that we shall not find Him? Does He intend to go to the Dispersion among the Greeks and teach the Greeks? 36 What is this thing that He said, 'You will seek Me and not find Me, and where I am you cannot come'?" 37 On the last day, that great day of the feast, Jesus stood and cried out, saying, "If anyone thirsts, let him come to Me and drink. 38 He who believes in Me, as the Scripture has said, out of his heart will flow rivers of living water." 39 But this He spoke concerning the Spirit, whom those believing in Him would receive; for the Holy Spirit was not yet given, because Jesus was not yet glorified.

Jesus is saying in essence, "I am Yahweh and I AM everything you need. I am Yeshua, the Salvation that you are calling for. Come to me and drink and never thirst again. I am the seventh Man, the Man of completion and the Man that will give rest for all the nations."

The word salvation in Hebrew is "Yeshua"; in Greek it is "sozo". Both mean forgiveness, deliverance, prosperity, victory, joy, happiness, peace, safety, wholeness.

Peace is the Hebrew word "shalom" –it also means forgiveness, deliverance, prosperity, victory, joy, happiness, peace, safety, wholeness.

Salvation is shalom and the Word says Yeshua is the Prince of Shalom!

Remember, God told Abraham, "Through you all nations will be blessed." The Jews call it the "Messianic Period." It represents when all nations will recognize the Messiah and gather in Jerusalem on Sukkot and will forever live under the blessing in every area of our lives!

Isaiah 2:2-3
Now it shall come to pass in the latter days that the mountain of the Lord's house shall be established on the top of the mountains, And shall be exalted above the hills; And all nations shall flow to it. 3 Many people shall come and say, "Come, and let us go up to the mountain of the Lord, to the house of the God of Jacob; He will teach us His ways, And we shall walk in His

paths." For out of Zion shall go forth the law (Torah), and the word of the Lord from Jerusalem.

The latter days speak of the millennial kingdom and reign of Christ. It will be during this time He will be again on the earth and teaching the Torah of God's instructions to all the Nations. Jew, Gentile & the Church will be hearing from the Living Word and the Holy Spirit as our teacher. It will be during this time that the Tabernacles Celebration will not be optional. Those who keep it will be abundantly blessed with showers of rain and blessing while those who don't will live without rain and blessing. If we are all going to be keeping this celebration in the millennium, then why would we not want to be like Jesus and do it now? Especially we don't have to; we get to!

Zechariah 14:4-9, 16-19
And in that day His feet will stand on the Mount of Olives, Which faces Jerusalem on the east. And the Mount of Olives shall be split in two, From east to west, Making a very large valley; Half of the mountain shall move toward the north And half of it toward the south. 5 Then you shall flee through My mountain valley, For the mountain valley shall reach to Azal. Yes, you shall flee As you fled from the earthquake In the days of Uzziah king of Judah. Thus the Lord my God will come, And all the saints with You. 6 It shall come to pass in that day That there will be no light; The lights will diminish. 7 It shall be one day Which is known to the Lord— Neither day nor night. But at

evening time it shall happen That it will be light. 8 And in that day it shall be That living waters shall flow from Jerusalem, Half of them toward the eastern sea And half of them toward the western sea; In both summer and winter it shall occur. 9 And the Lord shall be King over all the earth. In that day it shall be—"The Lord is one," And His name one. 16 And it shall come to pass that everyone who is left of all the nations which came against Jerusalem shall go up from year to year to worship the King, the Lord of hosts, and to keep the Feast of Tabernacles. 17 And it shall be that whichever of the families of the earth do not come up to Jerusalem to worship the King, the Lord of hosts, on them there will be no rain. 18 If the family of Egypt will not come up and enter in, they shall have no rain; they shall receive the plague with which the Lord strikes the nations who do not come up to keep the Feast of Tabernacles. 19 This shall be the punishment of Egypt and the punishment of all the nations that do not come up to keep the Feast of Tabernacles.

In the book of Acts the book of Amos is quoted as the proof that God wanted to extend grace and to save the nations. The Gentiles would no longer be strangers to the covenant, for God loves the stranger and the world. In Amos, the Tabernacle of David is actually the same word for Sukkah or booth.

The prophetic signs, type and shadows of the Feast of Nations point to God's heart for all people. We must remember as we keep and celebrate this feast to invite the strangers in and welcome them, they do not have to live like strangers anymore once they find out that God wants to be their Tabernacle. The greater spiritual identity is found as we look into the perfect law of liberty and see ourselves through its light.

Acts 15:11-17 NKJV
11 But we believe that through the grace of the Lord Jesus Christ we shall be saved in the same manner as they."12 Then all the multitude kept silent and listened to Barnabas and Paul declaring how many miracles and wonders God had worked through them among the Gentiles. 13 And after they had become silent, James answered, saying, "Men and brethren, listen to me: 14 Simon has declared how God at the first visited the Gentiles to take out of them a people for His name. 15 And with this the words of the prophets agree, just as it is written: 16 'After this I will return And will rebuild the tabernacle of David, which has fallen down; I will rebuild its ruins, And I will set it up; 17 So that the rest of mankind may seek the Lord, Even all the Gentiles who are called by My name, Says the Lord who does all these things.'

Amos 9:11-15 NKJB
11 "On that day I will raise up The tabernacle of David, which has fallen down, And repair its damages; I will raise up its ruins, And rebuild it as in the days of old; 12 That they may possess the remnant of Edom, And all

the Gentiles who are called by My name," Says the Lord who does this thing. 13 "Behold, the days are coming," says the Lord, "When the plowman shall overtake the reaper, And the treader of grapes him who sows seed; The mountains shall drip with sweet wine, And all the hills shall flow with it. 14 I will bring back the captives of My people Israel; They shall build the waste cities and inhabit them; They shall plant vineyards and drink wine from them; They shall also make gardens and eat fruit from them.15 I will plant them in their land, And no longer shall they be pulled up From the land I have given them, "Says the Lord your God.

It is time for the nations to know their inheritance and the invitation to come and drink of the Living Waters.

CHAPTER TWO:

Personal and Small Group Study

How many nations were in the time of Israel?

_____

How many bull were sacrificed on the Feast of
Nations_____

Leviticus 19:33-34 AMP
33 And if a _____ dwells temporarily
with you in your land, you shall not suppress and
_____ him.34 But the
_____ who dwells with you shall be to
you as one _____ among you; and you
shall _____ him as yourself, for you were
_____ in the land of Egypt. I am the
Lord your God.

At a certain time they would cry out, "Oh, God,
_____!" and the special
ceremony would take place. It is filled with
_____ and _____ of Jesus.

On _____, all priests in Jerusalem would
gather at the Temple. The _____ would
also be welcomed to come to the Temple during this
time. The priests and Levites who worked in the
Temple were then divided into _____distinct
groups.

What is the number ten symbolic of?
_____,
_____,
_____

According to John chapter three, why are men judged
already?

_____

_____

_____

_____

_____

_____

_____

The _____ would no longer be
_____ to the covenant for God loves the
stranger and the world. In Amos, the Tabernacle of
David is actually the same word for _____
or booth.

What is the number seventy symbolic of?

_____,
_____,
_____,
_____.

What does the tabernacle of David represent to those in
the book of Acts?

_____
_____
_____
_____
_____
_____
_____

On Tabernacles, what are the people praying for?

_____

Describe each of the four species and what they are
symbolic of.

CHAPTER THREE:

A Season of Rejoicing and Thanksgiving

Could it be possible that the Thanksgiving holiday in America was actually rooted in the Feast of Tabernacles? One of the names of this feast is actually the Season of Rejoicing and the Feast of Ingathering. It is harvest time that brings the greatest joy because the fruit of your hard work and labor are finally realized when the time of harvest has come.

Three of the Chagag, or "foot feasts" as they are sometimes known, required Israel to come to Jerusalem and celebrate and party during the three main harvests of the year. They were to come at the barley harvest during the Feast of Unleavened Bread, the wheat harvest at the Feast of Shavuot, and the fruit or wine harvest at that Feast of Tabernacles.

The final and seventh feast is sometimes referred to as the Feast of Ingathering. It is a promise of God's bounty and provision, much like was expected when the

Pilgrims came to America and celebrated their first harvest with a season of Thanksgiving as they gathered the fruit from the earth of the New World. I love to think that God has already programmed in His calendar, times of harvest, gathering and celebrations.

Exodus 23: 14-16
14 "Three times you shall keep a feast to Me in the year: 15 You shall keep the Feast of Unleavened Bread (you shall eat unleavened bread seven days, as I commanded you, at the time appointed in the month of Abib, for in it you came out of Egypt; none shall appear before Me empty); 16 and the Feast of Harvest, the firstfruits of your labors which you have sown in the field; and the Feast of Ingathering at the end of the year, when you have gathered in the fruit of your labors from the field.

Chagag: Celebrate, dance, keep, hold a solemn feast holiday, reel to and fro A primitive root (compare chagra', chuwg); properly, to move in a circle, i.e. (specifically) to march in a sacred procession, to observe a festival; by implication, to be giddy -- celebrate, dance, (keep, hold) a (solemn) feast (holiday), reel to and fro.

When Israel would go to Jerusalem on these Chagag, they would rejoice like there was no tomorrow! They were up all night partying, dancing, singing, praising and worshipping. It was a revival like we have never seen. There are no parties like the ones God invites us to, and Tabernacles was the biggest and greatest party of the year. It was seven days of rejoicing!

Deuteronomy 16: 13-17 NKHV
13 "You shall observe the Feast of Tabernacles seven days, when you have gathered from your threshing floor and from your winepress. 14 And you shall rejoice in your feast, you and your son and your daughter, your male servant and your female servant and the Levite, the stranger and the fatherless and the widow, who are within your gates. 15 Seven days you shall keep a sacred feast to the Lord your God in the place, which the Lord chooses, because the Lord your God will bless you in all your produce and in all the work of your hands, so that you surely rejoice. 16 "Three times a year all your males shall appear before the Lord your God in the place which He chooses: at the Feast of Unleavened Bread, at the Feast of Weeks, and at the Feast of Tabernacles; and they shall not appear before the Lord empty-handed. 17 Every man shall give as he is able, according to the blessing of the Lord your God which He has given you.
The rejoicing was not optional; it is actually commanded. And it is not just for Israel, but all who live there. We can see in this Moed the heart of God for those who are hurting or without the covenant being included so they can rejoice and have a harvest, too!

The blessing of God knows no bounds, for He sends His rain upon whoever is present to receive.

Thanksgiving in America was actually modeled by the Pilgrims after this feast. Thanksgiving was really another Sukkot! The Pilgrims called themselves "Old Testament Christians" or "Judeo-Christians." They believed they were pilgrims coming out of Europe and represented the Israelites coming out of Egypt.

They had left Europe so they could get away from the Roman Catholic Church and to be free to worship the God of Abraham, Isaac & Jacob.

As Hebrew Christians we get to keep and celebrate this season of harvest and are thankful to the One who provides and sustains us with His abundance.

King Solomon had celebrated the Feast and dedicated the Temple on this appointed day.

2 Chronicles 7:1-3
When Solomon had finished praying, fire came down from heaven and consumed the burnt offering and the sacrifices; and the glory of the Lord filled the temple. 2 And the priests could not enter the house of the Lord, because the glory of the Lord had filled the Lord's house. 3 When all the children of Israel saw how the fire came down, and the glory of the Lord on the temple, they bowed their faces to the ground on the

pavement, and worshiped and praised the Lord, saying: "For He is good, For His mercy endures forever."

Can you see how Solomon was syncing, harmonizing and connecting with God's divine calendar? Solomon is known for his wisdom that he received as a gift from God because of his humility. It was God who was guiding and instructing him to dedicate the Temple on Tabernacles. The Temple would be a place where the presence of the Lord would manifest and the entire world would see God's glory.

Solomon built a physical temple that would one day be destroyed. It was temporary and not permanent. It was, however, symbolic, for God would ultimately want to dwell in another temple; His people.

2 Chronicles 7:8-10 NKJV
8 At that time Solomon kept the feast seven days, and all Israel with him, a very great assembly from the entrance of Hamath to the Brook of Egypt. 9 And on the eighth day they held a sacred assembly, for they observed the dedication of the altar seven days, and the feast seven days. 10 On the twenty-third day of the seventh month he sent the people away to their tents, joyful and glad of heart for the good that the Lord had done for David, for Solomon, and for His people Israel.

At that time of Tabernacles the Temple was dedicated, just like our temple should be dedicated to and for the Lord's glory, for we belong to Him. As we dedicate our temple to Him, we should rejoice for all the good we have seen from the Lord.

1 Corinthians 6:19-20
19 Or do you not know that your body is the temple of the Holy Spirit who is in you, whom you have from God, and you are not your own? 20 For you were bought at a price; therefore glorify God in your body and in your spirit, which are God's.

The temple of the Holy Spirit is now our impermanent bodies, which are a type of booth and tabernacle that carry God's presence wherever, we may go. The born again and Kingdom believers now have the privilege of having the Light of the world inside of us.

God appeared to Solomon two times. At the last encounter He gave him promises and a warning for what would happen to the Temple if Solomon and his descendants did not follow the Lord's instructions.

1 Kings 9:1-9 NKJV
And it came to pass, when Solomon had finished building the house of the Lord and the king's house, and all Solomon's desire which he wanted to do, 2 that the Lord appeared to Solomon the second time, as He

had appeared to him at Gibeon. 3 And the Lord said to him: "I have heard your prayer and your supplication that you have made before Me; I have consecrated this house which you have built to put My name there forever, and My eyes and My heart will be there perpetually. 4 Now if you walk before Me as your father David walked, in integrity of heart and in uprightness, to do according to all that I have commanded you, and if you keep My statutes and My judgments, 5 then I will establish the throne of your kingdom over Israel forever, as I promised David your father, saying, 'You shall not fail to have a man on the throne of Israel.' 6 But if you or your sons at all turn from following Me, and do not keep My commandments and My statutes which I have set before you, but go and serve other gods and worship them, 7 then I will cut off Israel from the land which I have given them; and this house which I have consecrated for My name I will cast out of My sight. Israel will be a proverb and a byword among all peoples. 8 And as for this house, which is exalted, everyone who passes by it will be astonished and will hiss, and say, 'Why has the Lord done thus to this land and to this house?' 9 Then they will answer, 'Because they forsook the Lord their God, who brought their fathers out of the land of Egypt, and have embraced other gods, and worshiped them and served them; therefore the Lord has brought all this calamity on them.' "

Solomon, like many today, started out good, but allowed things to enter and cloud his judgment and behavior. Hopefully we will learn from reading and looking at the examples of those who went before us.

1 Kings 9:25 NKJV
25 Now three times a year Solomon offered burnt offerings and peace offerings on the altar, which he had built for the Lord, and he burned incense with them on the altar that was before the Lord. So he finished the temple.

There is a great promise I found that is obscure in the book of Nahum. The promise is for those who will keep and celebrate those divine appointments. When Judah would keep these feasts, God promised that the devil would be cut off and no longer pass through their land. Wow! Wouldn't that be awesome if we did not have to deal with Satan and his schemes any longer?

Nahum 1:15 Jubilee Bible 2000
Behold upon the mountains the feet of him that brings good tidings, of him that publishes peace! O Judah, keep thy solemn feasts, perform thy vows; for Belial shall no longer pass through thee; he is utterly cut off.

According to the Torah Scriptures, you will find that first fruit offerings were to be given three times a year and that the males would go to Jerusalem. There were to be love offerings and the males would bless the Lord according to their abilities and what the Lord had already blessed them with. The offering was a response of love and thanksgiving to the Lord for His provision and sustenance.

My wife and I have begun to follow this principle and have seen great blessing since we have done this. We also attach our faith to the offering for something particular. God desires, not to take from us, but get blessing to us.

The heart of all of God's Feasts draws us closer to Him so He can remind us of who we are and of our inheritance of abundance in Him. There is much we can learn about the Torah way for giving and finances, which we will hopefully pen another time. For now, understand this is a season to rejoice and be thankful. God is a good God; He wants to bless you so you can be a light and blessing in the earth. SEND NOW PROSPERITY!

CHAPTER THREE:

Personal and Small Group Study

What does the Hebrew word Chagag mean and what were the three times of year that Israel was to go to Jerusalem?

_____

_____

_____

_____

_____

_____

_____

_____

_____

_____

_____

_____

The final and _____ feast is sometimes referred to the Feast of _____ which is a promise of God's _____and provision, much like was expected when the _____ came to America and celebrated there first harvest with a season of _____ as they _____the fruit from the earth of the New World.

The _____ called themselves Old Testament _____ or Judeo-_____. They believed they were _____ coming out of Europe and represented _____ coming out of Egypt.

There are no _____ like the ones God invites us to, and _____ was the biggest and greatest _____ of the year. It was _____ days of _____!

The temple of the Holy Spirit is now our _____ bodies, which are a type of _____ and tabernacle that carry God's presence wherever we may go. The born again and _____ believers now have the privilege of having the Light of the world _____ of us.

How many times did God appear to King Solomon?

_____

Deuteronomy 16:13-14
13 "You shall observe the Feast of Tabernacles _____ days, when you have _____ from your threshing floor and from your _____. 14 And you shall _____ in your feast, you and your son and your daughter, your male servant and your female servant and the Levite, the _____ and the _____ and the widow, who are within your _____.

Solomon built a _____ temple that would one day be _____. It was temporary and not _____. It was, however, symbolic, for God would ultimately want to _____ in another temple, which is His _____.

Give some reasons that Solomon's Temple was destroyed?

_____

_____

_____

_____

_____

_____

According to Nahum, what is the promise to those who keep the appointed feasts?

_____

_____

_____

_____

_____

_____

_____

1 Corinthians 6:19-20

19 Or do you not know that your body is the
_____ of the Holy Spirit who is in you, whom
you have from God, and you are not your _____?
20 For you were bought at a price; therefore
_____ God in your _____ and in your
spirit, which are _____.

CHAPTER FOUR:

The Birth of Christ

Today it seems so much of the world loves the time of Christmas. We hear the beautiful songs, the decorations of lights and trees and the shopping for gifts that has become a great part of culture. Christmas is not just for Christians anymore!

I remember growing up Jewish. I felt left out until my mother remarried a Catholic man who brought the Christmas tree and traditions to our home. We had a Hanukkah menorah and a Christmas tree in the same room. I was happy because I never got so many presents. Even after my Mom was divorced we still kept the tradition. I, too, had kept the tradition after I had become a Christian at fifteen and married by nineteen to my wife, Lisa, who was the granddaughter of the pastor of my church. We loved Christmastime because it was so much fun, especially when we had a daughter of our own. We could shower her with abundant presents.

For many years I never knew what I am going to do my best to show you from the Scriptures. Did you know that Jesus was not born on December 25th? Now, I know you might have heard that, but would you want your birthday celebrated the wrong day? Would God want His people honoring the wrong day when He had the right day in the Word the whole time? I don't think so and I know you don't either. So, if we are going to honor Jesus on His birthday, then let's find out when that really was.

Proverbs 25:2 APBE
It is the glory of God that hides the word, and the glory of the King that seeks for the word.

We are the kings who have the privilege and blessing to search the Scriptures, for they will be our evidence and confirmation of all that Jesus is and came for.

One of the reasons for the Moedim is that they are prophetic pictures of past, present and future events. As you begin to look at God's calendar, you will find that each of them is confirmed and has great value in the scheme and plan of God. Shadows point to a reality, and so even these Feasts point to the reality of Christ.

The Feast of Tabernacles is the time that I believe Scripture points to as the real birth of Messiah, Jesus.

The first day of the Feast was His day of birth, and the separate, but connected eighth day was His circumcision.
Both the first and eighth days were considered to be High Sabbaths.

A High Sabbath is an appointed day in the Moedim that was to be honored and a marked as an additional Sabbath. Jesus is Lord of the Sabbath and the Sabbath is the Lord's Day according to Isaiah chapter fifty-eight.

When Jesus was born, the day of His birth confirmed Him as the True Rest for the people of God when we simply receive the blessing of grace He came to bring. Not only was Jesus born on the first day of Sukkot, but He also lived in a Sukkah for the first seven days of His birth, which was a requirement of the Torah.

Think of how this corresponds and will complement what we have already learned about what Tabernacles is. This time on God's calendar reminds us that God is our Provider, Sustainer, Protector and the Source of all blessing and good.

We already know this Tabernacles time is also known as the Feast of Nations. So when the angel announces Jesus birth, what does he say?

Luke 2:8-14 NKJV

8 Now there were in the same country shepherds living out in the fields, keeping watch over their flock by night. 9 And behold, an angel of the Lord stood before them, and the glory of the Lord shone around them, and they were greatly afraid. 10 Then the angel said to them, "Do not be afraid, for behold, I bring you good tidings of great joy which will be to all people. 11 For there is born to you this day in the city of David a Savior, who is Christ the Lord. 12 And this will be the sign to you: You will find a Babe wrapped in swaddling cloths, lying in a manger." 13 And suddenly there was with the angel a multitude of the heavenly host praising God and saying: 14 "Glory to God in the highest, And on earth peace, goodwill toward men!"

The angel takes the announcement to the shepherds, who must have been near the place of Jesus' birth in Bethlehem; the place prophesied of Messiah's birth. What is the multitude of hosts announcing into the atmosphere on the Feast of Nations? They're saying the good news of the gospel has come to bring joy to all people. The angels are announcing the gospel to the Nations and Gentiles who didn't have a covenant.

When they said "all people", they were also referring to the lost scattered sheep of the house of Israel; those who were swallowed up and became Gentiles when they were broken and loosed from their covenant of marriage with Yahweh in their rebellion, stubbornness and idolatry.

It was during the Feast of Nations that the angels announced the message of shalom, peace and goodwill towards all the descendants of Adam. Since we know that, on the Feast of Tabernacles, the nations were welcomed and encouraged to participate and be included in this Feast, it makes sense that the angels announced Jesus' birth on Tabernacles for the wholeness of all people. Righteousness and peace have kissed and Jesus' birth will be the confirmation of the heart of God to bring mercy and truth together.

John 1:14 YLT
And the Word became flesh, and did tabernacle among us, and we beheld his glory, glory as of an only begotten of a father, full of grace and truth.

The Apostle John has penned for us, by the Holy Spirit, that Jesus came and "tabernacled" among us. Would Jesus come to be our Tabernacle and not be born on the Tabernacle Feast? Since the Moedim are confirmations, why would Jesus not be born as the goal, point and fullest expression of what Tabernacles really means?

If we want to honor Jesus' birth, shouldn't we be doing it on the right day, when He came and "tabernacled" among us? Since when is tradition or culture greater or more important than keeping God's Word?

No person can orchestrate the time of their birth, yet Christ was born at the fullness and right time that all the

Scriptures confirm. Even the stars confirmed the location and birth of Christ.

In the book of Revelations we see that, on the eighth day of new beginnings, which is, that last and extra day connected to this Feast, we see God coming to "tabernacle" again among us. I am sure that day will also be during this Feast.

Can you see how Tabernacles is a picture of Christ's birth?

Revelation 21:1-4
Now I saw a new heaven and a new earth, for the first heaven and the first earth had passed away. Also there was no more sea. 2 Then I, John, saw the holy city, New Jerusalem, coming down out of heaven from God, prepared as a bride adorned for her husband. 3 And I heard a loud voice from heaven saying, "Behold, the tabernacle of God is with men, and He will dwell with them, and they shall be His people. God Himself will be with them and be their God. 4 And God will wipe away every tear from their eyes; there shall be no more death, nor sorrow, nor crying. There shall be no more pain, for the former things have passed away."

Let's now look at the birth of Christ as written in the Scriptures and see if we can discover more.

Luke 1:5-44

5 There was in the days of Herod, the king of Judea, a certain priest named Zacharias, of the division of Abijah. His wife was of the daughters of Aaron, and her name was Elizabeth. 6 And they were both righteous before God, walking in all the commandments and ordinances of the Lord blameless. 7 But they had no child, because Elizabeth was barren, and they were both well advanced in years. 8 So it was, that while he was serving as priest before God in the order of his division, 9 according to the custom of the priesthood, his lot fell to burn incense when he went into the temple of the Lord. 10 And the whole multitude of the people was praying outside at the hour of incense. 11 Then an angel of the Lord appeared to him, standing on the right side of the altar of incense. 12 And when Zacharias saw him, he was troubled, and fear fell upon him. 13 But the angel said to him, "Do not be afraid, Zacharias, for your prayer is heard; and your wife Elizabeth will bear you a son, and you shall call his name John. 14 And you will have joy and gladness, and many will rejoice at his birth. 15 For he will be great in the sight of the Lord, and shall drink neither wine nor strong drink. He will also be filled with the Holy Spirit, even from his mother's womb. 16 And he will turn many of the children of Israel to the Lord their God. 17 He will also go before Him in the spirit and power of Elijah, 'to turn the hearts of the fathers to the children,' and the disobedient to the wisdom of the just, to make ready a people prepared for the Lord." 18 And Zacharias said to the angel, "How shall I know this? For I am an old man, and my wife is well advanced in years."19 And the

angel answered and said to him, "I am Gabriel, who stands in the presence of God, and was sent to speak to you and bring you these glad tidings. 20 But behold, you will be mute and not able to speak until the day these things take place, because you did not believe my words which will be fulfilled in their own time." 21 And the people waited for Zacharias, and marveled that he lingered so long in the temple. 22 But when he came out, he could not speak to them; and they perceived that he had seen a vision in the temple, for he beckoned to them and remained speechless.23 So it was, as soon as the days of his service were completed, that he departed to his own house. 24 Now after those days his wife Elizabeth conceived; and she hid herself five months, saying, 25 "Thus the Lord has dealt with me, in the days when He looked on me, to take away my reproach among people."26 Now in the sixth month the angel Gabriel was sent by God to a city of Galilee named Nazareth, 27 to a virgin betrothed to a man whose name was Joseph, of the house of David. The virgin's name was Mary. 28 And having come in, the angel said to her, "Rejoice, highly favored one, the Lord is with you; blessed are you among women!"29 But when she saw him, she was troubled at his saying, and considered what manner of greeting this was. 30 Then the angel said to her, "Do not be afraid, Mary, for you have found favor with God. 31 And behold, you will conceive in your womb and bring forth a Son, and shall call His name Jesus. 32 He will be great, and will be called the Son of the Highest; and the Lord God will give Him the throne of His father David. 33 And He will reign over the house of Jacob forever, and of His kingdom there will be no end."34 Then Mary said to the angel, "How can this be, since I do not know a man?" 35 And the angel answered and said to her, "The Holy Spirit will come upon you, and the power of the Highest will overshadow you; therefore, also, that Holy One who is to be born will be called the Son of God. 36 Now indeed, Elizabeth your relative has also conceived a son in her old age; and this is now the sixth month for her who was called barren. 37 For with God nothing will be impossible."38 Then Mary said, "Behold the maidservant of the Lord! Let it be to me according to your word." And the angel departed from her.39 Now Mary arose in those days and went into the hill country with haste, to a city of Judah, 40 and entered the house of Zacharias and greeted Elizabeth. 41 And it happened, when Elizabeth heard the greeting of Mary, that the babe leaped in her womb; and Elizabeth was filled with the Holy Spirit. 42 Then she spoke out with a loud voice and said, "Blessed are you among women, and blessed is the fruit of your womb! 43 But why is this granted to me, that the mother of my Lord should come to me? 44 For indeed, as soon as the voice of your greeting sounded in my ears, the babe leaped in my womb for joy.

If you read this carefully, you will find that Jesus' and John's birth are actually connected. Why would this be true? Because Jesus will be the One who will be the Prophet like Moses that the people will hear, and John will be the one who comes in the Spirit of Elijah, according to the angel, to prepare the way for Yeshua Messiah.

Elizabeth had been barren like the matriarchs who required a miracle to have their appointed children, but after an encounter with the angel Gabriel in the Temple during his appointed time of service, Zacharias goes home and Elizabeth gets pregnant.

The eighth division of Abijah served in the Temple during the tenth and thirty fourth weeks of the year. This was Zacharias' priestly duty at this time. He also would have been serving at Shavuot/Pentecost, most likely in May or June, during the month of Sivan. That is when Elizabeth conceived.

By the time Mary arrived in November or December, the Hebrew month of Kislev, Elizabeth was six months pregnant with John. The time is Hanukkah, the Festival of Lights. This is when Christ was miraculously conceived as the Light of the world.

Mary visits Elizabeth and the Holy Spirit fills John in his mother's womb. Mary has her own personal encounter with the Holy Spirit during the Hanukkah season and stays with her cousin for three months.

Remember, the birth of Jesus is tied to John's birth. The clues in Scripture show us that John was born three months after Hanukkah, which means John will be born during the time of Passover. A tradition in the Passover

Seder is to set a place of Elijah at the table and open the door to let the spirit of Elijah come in, because he prepares the way for Messiah.

Jesus said that John was the greatest prophet who ever lived.

Matthew 11:14 NASB
"And if you are willing to accept it, John himself is Elijah who was to come.

John is six months older than Jesus. If John is born at Passover, during the Spring Feasts, then Jesus would be born at Tabernacles, during the Fall Feasts.

Let's look at some more scripture about Messiah's birth.

Luke 2:1-7
And it came to pass in those days that a decree went out from Caesar Augustus that all the world should be registered. 2 This census first took place while Quirinius was governing Syria. 3 So all went to be registered, everyone to his own city. 4 Joseph also went up from Galilee, out of the city of Nazareth, into Judea, to the city of David, which is called Bethlehem, because he was of the house and lineage of David, 5 to be registered with Mary, his betrothed wife, who was with child. 6 So it was, that while they were there, the days were completed for her to be delivered. 7 And she

brought forth her firstborn Son, and wrapped Him in swaddling cloths, and laid Him in a manger, because there was no room for them in the inn.

Look at verse 2:
2 This was the first census taken before Quirinius was governor of Syria.

Biblical scholars have been skeptical about this census, saying Luke made an error in the timing of the census, BUT the Greek word prote/protos, usually translated "first" can also be translated "prior" or "before."

The best time to take a count of people would be when the people are all gathered together. Since Tabernacles is a Chagag, a required time to gather together at Jerusalem, the census was decreed during Sukkot/Tabernacles. The local dwellers would build the booths for those visiting.

Joseph and Mary were pregnant and the long journey from Nazareth to Bethlehem was sixty-nine miles. The first born was given back to the Lord as a first fruit offering and Mary and Joseph would have brought their son, who was named Yeshua by the angel, to the Temple as this first fruit offering and also to be dedicated according to the Torah.

So, where was Jesus actually born? We know that at His birth He was wrapped in "swaddling clothes", which were the linen robes of the priests that were saved after they had become aged or damaged.
He was also laid in a manger, which was actually a feeding trough for the cattle or animals. This was prophetic as Jesus would be the feeder and give nourishment to the world.

Do you remember how we read the angels first came to the shepherds who were in the field watching over their flocks? In Bethlehem these were not ordinary shepherds, but they were of the priestly order given the task of making sure the newborn lambs were clean and unblemished; holy and worthy for the atonement offerings.

In the fields, the shepherds had built towers, called migdal in Hebrew. These towers were made of stone. They were simple structures with a watchtower on top so the shepherds could keep watch over and protect their flocks. They would also use them for the birthing of the baby lambs. When a female lamb was about to give birth, she was taken to the base of this tower where there was a room where she could deliver her lambs on the stone floor. This was kept ritualistically clean in case a qualified Paschal lamb might be born. This migdal also had a manger, a food crib or animal feeding trough that was made of hewn stone.

After their birth, what do you think the lambs were wrapped in? When a spotless lamb was born, he was actually wrapped in "swaddling clothes", the linen priestly garments that were on hand for these special lambs. He was then placed in the clean manger until he settled himself, so that he would not thrash and break a bone or injure himself and incur a blemish.

In Hebrew the word Migdal Eder means "Tower of the Flock". It is actually talked about in the Scriptures in light of the King and Messiah.

Micah 4:8
And you, O tower of the flock, The stronghold of the daughter of Zion,
To you shall it come, Even the former dominion shall come, The kingdom of the daughter of Jerusalem."

The shepherds would have recognized the words of the angel as a sign pointing them to the Migdal Eder, Tower of the Flock, because this was the only place where something would be "swaddled in clothes" and "lying a manger".

Because Bethlehem was known for being the place where prime sheep were bred for the Temple sacrifices, the Bethlehem shepherds were not ordinary shepherds. They were Levitical priests who were specifically trained to recognize the sacrificial lambs and to raise them healthy and safe from injury.

So, could Jesus have been born in the Tower of the Flock? What did John call Jesus when he saw Him coming to be baptized? John refers to Jesus two times as the Lamb of God.

John 1: 29-35 NKJV
29 The next day John saw Jesus coming toward him, and said, "Behold! The Lamb of God who takes away the sin of the world! 30 This is He of whom I said, 'After me comes a Man who is preferred before me, for He was before me.' 31 I did not know Him; but that He should be revealed to Israel, therefore I came baptizing with water." 32 And John bore witness, saying, "I saw the Spirit descending from heaven like a dove, and He remained upon Him. 33 I did not know Him, but He who sent me to baptize with water said to me, 'Upon whom you see the Spirit descending, and remaining on Him, this is He who baptizes with the Holy Spirit.' 34 And I have seen and testified that this is the Son of God." 35 Again, the next day, John stood with two of his disciples. 36 And looking at Jesus as He walked, he said, "Behold the Lamb of God!"

I think we should be celebrating the birth of Christ. We have the specific accounts of Matthew and Luke that tell us of this important event. We have searched the Scriptures and can conclude, with no doubt that Jesus was not born on December 25th. That day is not a Moed!

God has chosen prophetically appointed days to meet with Him, to be reminded of our past and rehearse for what is to come. We must be careful not to commit the sin of Jeroboam, who made a false holy day and two places that were more convenient for Israel to worship to keep them from the real thing.

The true spirit of Christmas will only be found when we are humble enough to get in sync with God's calendar and His traditions. If you see something in God's Word, don't fight it or reject it. The Word is forever settled and will not change. We must conform our ways to it, and not the other way around.

Jeremiah 16:19 GW
The Lord is my strength and my fortress, my refuge in times of trouble. Nations come to you from the most distant parts of the world and say, "Our ancestors have inherited lies, worthless and unprofitable gods."

Jeremiah is talking about Israel who will be swallowed up by the nations. They will become the nations, and even when they come to Jesus, they will bring with them the lies that they have inherited, but are useless, for they are not founded in the truth of God's Word and Torah instructions.

Jesus echoes the word of the prophet Jeremiah.

Matthew 15:6-9 PT

6 This doesn't honor your father or mother. And you have elevated your tradition above the words of God. 7 Frauds and hypocrites! Isaiah described you perfectly when he said: 8 These people honor me only with their words, for their hearts are so very distant from me.9 They pretend to worship me, but their worship is nothing more than the empty traditions of men."

As we close this book, remember that Tabernacles reminds us not to put our trust in anything but God and His Word. No tradition, no person, no culture or religion can be more important that honoring Him.

Jesus is the Tabernacle. In Him we are safe and secure from all harm. Always be willing to change when He asks. Don't let anything become an idol, even if it's Christmas because Jesus was born on this appointed day of Tabernacles.

CHAPTER FOUR:

Personal and Small Group Study

John is _____months older than Jesus and if John is born at _____during the Spring Feasts, then Jesus would be born at _____ during the Fall Feasts.

Proverbs 25:2 APBE
It is the glory of God that _____ the word, and the glory of the King that seeks for the

_____.

Jeremiah 16:19 GW
The Lord is my strength and my _____,
my refuge in times of trouble. _____
come to you from the most distant parts of the world
and say, "Our ancestors have inherited _____,
worthless and _____ gods."

Matthew 11:14 NASB
"And if you are willing to accept it, John himself is
_____ who was to come.

Describe what is a Tower of the Flock?

_____
_____
_____
_____
_____
_____
_____

John 1: 29
29 The next day John saw _____ coming
toward him, and said, "Behold! The _____
of God who takes away the _____ of the world!

What are "swaddling clothes" and where do they come
from?

_____
_____
_____
_____
_____
_____
_____

What is a manger and what is it made out of?

_____

_____

_____

_____

_____

_____

Matthew 15:6-9 PT
 6 This doesn't _____ your father or mother.
And you have elevated your _____ above
the words of God. 7 Frauds and hypocrites! Isaiah
described you perfectly when he said: 8 These people
honor me only with their _____, for their
hearts are so very distant from me.9 They
_____ to worship me, but their worship is
nothing more than the empty _____ of
men."

What did the angel Gabriel announce to the shepherds
and into the atmosphere?

_____

_____

_____

_____

_____

About the Author

Kenneth "Ken" Albin was born in New York, but moved to Florida as a young seven-year-old. Shortly after moving, Ken's parents were divorced, which left him deeply hurt for many years. During this time Ken, being Jewish, went to Hebrew school and Temple regularly. At the time of his thirteenth birthday and Bar Mitzvah, many confirmed a calling as a "rabbi" or "cantor" on his life.

It was soon after this that Ken's grandparents met the Lord at a Full Gospel businessmen's meeting. With momentum that came from above, Ken's father, David accepted the Lord, Jesus as his Savior. Being moved by his father's "born again" experience, Ken was now himself open to hear the message that so radically changed his dad's life. In the summer of Ken's sophomore year of high school, he gave his life to Jesus and his life was radically altered. He has been faithful to the house of God ever since. His mother, Racquel had also accepted Jesus and was now serving the Lord full time in Messianic ministry with her new husband, Rabbi Charles Kluge.

Ken has served in various areas of ministry including children's ministry, youth ministry and music ministry. He also has served in both associate and senior pastor roles for over twenty years. He has earned his Bachelor of Theology from International Seminary and his Master's Degree from Liberty University. He is also an accomplished singer/songwriter who has written over 100 songs. He loves to worship with the guitar and the keyboard.

Ken met his wife, Lisa at her grandfather's church in Margate, Florida. They were married when Lisa was just eighteen years of age. Six years later they welcomed their only child, Brittney into the world. Today Brittney and her husband, A.J. serve with Ken and Lisa in ministry and have a beautiful daughter, Brielle.

Ken and Lisa founded Save the Nations Church along with a handful of committed people who gathered in a home on September 17, 2006. God had put a vision in their hearts to reach the nations and bring light to a hurting world. Ken and Lisa currently serve as the overseeing pastors of the South Florida church campus in Broward County. As founders and pastors, they desire to inspire, instruct, resource and help people discover the destiny God has for them. The nations have become their home as together they travel to the nations, teaching, reviving and sharing the resources that help make influential disciples and bring people into appreciation of God's Torah, His "instructions."

Ken has always preached the word with the inspiration and revelation of the Holy Spirit. He has recently been on a journey to bring Christians into an understanding of the roots of their faith. "The Christian church has been hacked!" as Ken states in one of his latest books about restoring the inheritance and identity back to the church.

Presently, there are two international Save the Nations churches in Brazil: one in Rio and one in Marica'. Brazilian pastors, Diego and Kelly are doing an amazing work for God and great fruit is seen in that nation.

Ken has authored many books. All are available on Amazon. They are also being translated to Spanish, Portuguese and Russian languages.

BOOKS BY KENNETH S. ALBIN

YOU ARE BORN FOR THE EXTRAORDINARY

UPSIDE OF DOWN

THE MYSTERY OF THE CROWN

HACKED: THE HEBREW CHRISTIAN

THE PASSOVER BLESSING

NO MORE LEAVEN

HIT THE MARK

HIDDEN BLESSINGS REVEALED

HANUKKAH AND PURIM ARE FOR CHRISTIANS TOO!

Contact Information: for Ken & Lisa Albin
www.savethenations.com / www.hitthemarktorah.tv
info@savethenations.com

HANNUKAH
and PURIM
ARE FOR CHRISTIANS TOO!

KENNETH S. ALBIN

Christians

GET TO CELEBRATE

Passover

TOO!

Learning its Secrets, Power
and Abundant Blessings

KENNETH S. ALBIN

HOW INTENTIONALLY GOING LOWER CAN TAKE YOU HIGHER

UPSIDE OF DOWN

FOREWORD BY
DR. MARK
CHIRONNA

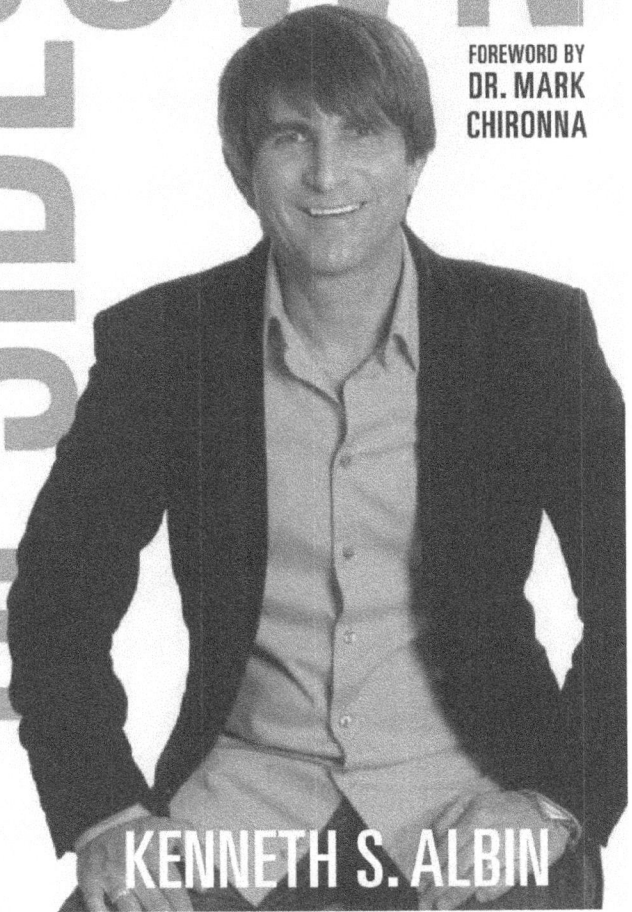

KENNETH S. ALBIN

HACKED

זהרת פריצה

RESTORING
STOLEN IDENTITY
AND EMBRACING THE
INHERITED BLESSING

THE HEBREW
CHRISTIAN

THE MYSTERY

OF THE CROWN

"WHY CHRIST HAD TO RECEIVE IT &
HOW ITS SECRETS CAN CHANGE YOUR WORLD."

FOREWORD BY TED SHUTTLESWORTH

KENNETH STEVEN ALBIN

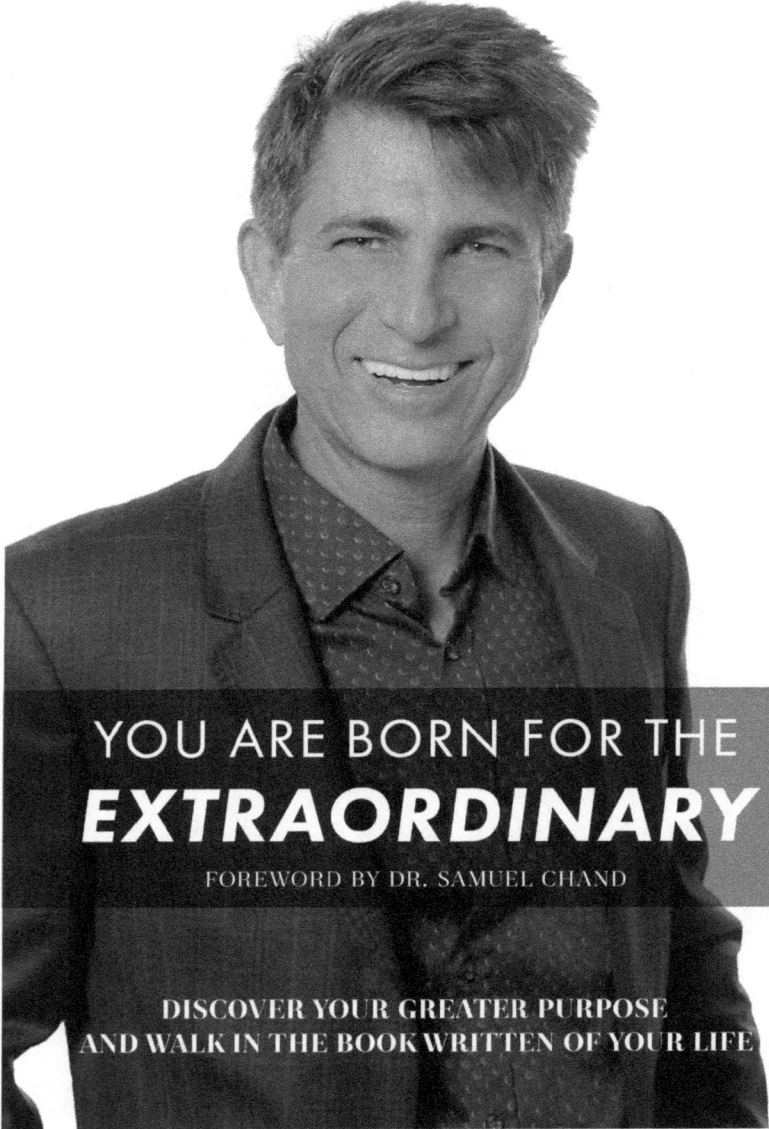

YOU ARE BORN FOR THE
EXTRAORDINARY

FOREWORD BY DR. SAMUEL CHAND

DISCOVER YOUR GREATER PURPOSE
AND WALK IN THE BOOK WRITTEN OF YOUR LIFE

No More Leaven!

The Blessings Christians Receive By Celebrating The Feast Of Unleavened Bread

By Kenneth S. Albin

HIT THE MARK

How Christians can
walk in the mysteries
of the Torah

And receive
all its blessings

HEALTH

ABUNDANT LIFE

PURPOSE-HAPPINESS-PEACE

Kenneth S. Albin

THE
BLESSINGS
OF
PENTECOST

לא תרצח
לא תנאף
לא תגנב
לא תענה
לא תחמד
אנכי ה'
לא יהיה
לא תשא
זכור את
כבד את

KENNETH S. ALBIN

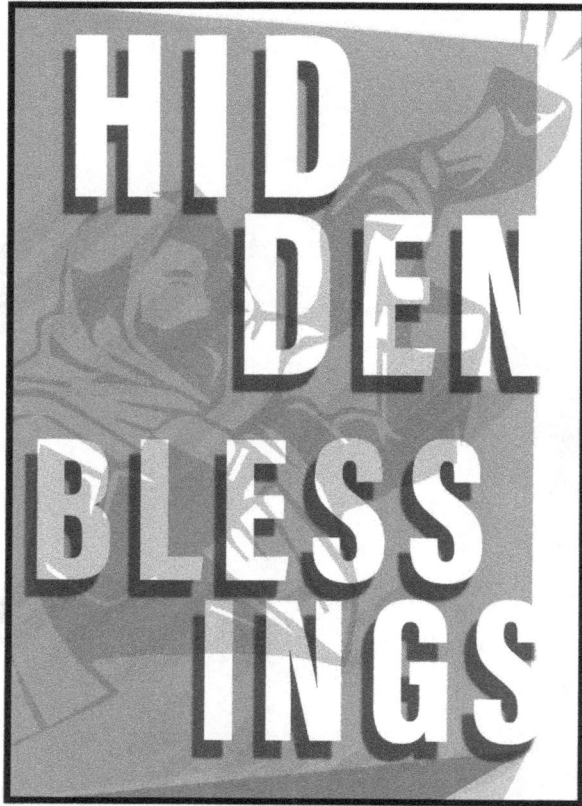

HID DEN BLESS INGS

REVEALED

A Christian Understanding for Celebrating
the Biblical Holidays of Rosh Hashanah and Yom Kippur

BY KENNETH S. ALBIN

www.ingramcontent.com/pod-product-compliance
Lightning Source LLC
LaVergne TN
LVHW011337080426
835513LV00006B/401